SOUL INFUSION GUIDE
A 6-Step Guide to Uplifting Your Life

Fenesha Hubbard

DEDICATION

For your soul, uplifted.

TABLE OF CONTENTS

DISCLAIMER

The content contained in this book is for informational purposes only. The reader accepts sole responsibility for the use of this content. The author cannot be held responsible for the way in which this information is applied.

Please respect the intellectual property of this work by not altering the content.   You may share this guide with others.   If you are inspired after reading the Soul Infusion Guide, please uplift a sisterfriend and share this book with her.   You are also welcome to post it online at a blog or other website with a link to its source and/or author website.

Thank you for respecting this work.

Dear Reader,

I'm Fenesha Hubbard, and I am a teacher and powerful manifesting vessel of wisdom and empowerment. I teach women how to say YES to themselves by cultivating their power within. In their experiences with me, women learn to create and cultivate habits of mind and spirit that will uplift their life. Cultivating habits of mind (what I consider the left brain) and spirit (what I loosely consider the right brain) require fully utilizing our gifts, talents and abilities.

When the left brain meets the right brain, you have me. I've always been the person who could objectively see situations, and subjectively create solutions. Today I bring over a decade of experience serving as a middle school math teacher, instructional coach, professional development facilitator, women's life coach, college lecturer, and self-care consultant to my life's work.

Sometimes titles make people feel secure enough to trust you, so suffice it to say that I've earned a BS in Mathematics, a MEd in Instructional Leadership, and a Compass Life Coach Certification. I offer a unique blend of my teaching and coaching experience to my clients, along with a personal philosophy rooted in spirituality.

I am transforming communities– one woman at a time. I work with women ready for change. I welcome you on this journey.

To your uplifting,

Fenesha

This Soul Infusion Guide is about saying YES to yourself. The 6-step process will give you practical steps to cultivate your power within. It's a guidebook based on the Universal Laws. Each step is followed by a prompt for your REFLECTION, an INFUSION STEP, which is an action to help you develop habits of mind, and an AFFIRMATION to support you.

EXPECTATIONS

If you are reading this book in hopes that it gives you a quick fix answer, then you will be disappointed. Change takes time. To cultivate the power within you, you've got to do the work. The seed was already planted, and that is why you're here, right now, in this moment. You must decide how much effort you are wiling to put forth to change your life. Just as I expect my clients to show up for themselves, I expect you, the reader, to do the same. You are the most important person in your life and if you cannot commit to yourself, then perhaps you are not ready... yet.

This book will serve as a beacon of light for your soul, if you are open and receptive. Are you ready? Let's GROW!

"Saying yes to myself is, by far, the hardest thing I've ever done." -Rising Sign Leo

You are the most important person in your life. How does that statement resonate with you? Does it feel good? Or do you have reservations about it? Perhaps you immediately thought of the other people in your life that you love and care for, because they are important to you. Or maybe you agree, and you want to learn to say YES to you more often.

Think about a woman you know who says YES to herself. She is radiant! You look at her and think, "Wow, she's doing her thing!" This woman is comfortable in her own skin and has the courage to march to her own beat. Her presence simply gives other people permission to let their light shine. Is that woman you?

How do you say YES to yourself? Who are you when you are Your Empowered Self? What is seeking to emerge from you? Are you willing to change? What must you let go so that you can grow? You will explore the answers to these questions as you complete the exercises in this book.

If you are truly ready to uplift your life, then you must be willing to face the truth of who you are and where you are right now.

The world desperately needs women to say YES to themselves. This book is the beginning of a call to action.

Let me introduce you to some of the women who might be reading this book, Playing It Safe Portia, Conflicted Chandra, and Tuned Out Tracey.

PLAYING IT SAFE PORTIA

"My life looks wonderful from the outside. Everyone thinks I've had a breakthrough, but the truth is I'm about to breakdown!"

CONFLICTED CHANDRA

"I want to uplift my life but there's no time! I've got so much going on with work and family that I can't find time in my schedule for me. I feel depleted but I've got to do this work because no one else will!"

TUNED OUT TRACEY

"Everyone has their opinion about what I should be doing with my life and I feel like I'm pleasing everyone but myself. I'm tuned into everyone's radio station and drained from all that static."

Do you know either of these women? (Perhaps one of them is you.) Each of these women has their own unique and personal journey, but one thing they have in common is that at some point they stopped saying YES to themselves.

This book is for all women ready and willing to say YES to their empowered self.

TRANSFORM your life! CULTIVATE your power within! LIVE with passion!

I'm just playing it safe in this game of life.

Playing it safe may mean that you earned that degree because your family told you that's where you'd earn a decent living. Or perhaps you chose a particular path because all of your friends were doing it, and it seemed like the right thing to do (although something deep down inside said it wasn't your time). No matter the situation, you love the life you live because of the opportunities it has afforded you. From the outside your life is picture perfect. However, on the inside there is conflict because you feel like you're living for someone else. You are ready to start living a more purposeful life.

WHAT YOUR ISSUES TEND TO BE

Days and weeks go by where you're on the grind, making things happen and having a great time. But after a while you start to have a physical breakdown. Maybe it's the constant headaches or the fatigue, but these things keep happening and it makes you pick up the phone and call your doctor (who tells you it's stress). You feel like you need to rest, and feel like your spirit is trying to tell you something. You know that if you keep playing it safe and keep ignoring your spirit, you're going to have a spiritual rock bottom experience. And the last thing you want to do is fall apart, especially because your life looks so damn good.

WHAT YOU NEED MOST RIGHT NOW

Your primary focus needs to be on you. It is time for you to say YES to you and feel good about your choices. It's time to trust life. You've controlled everything up to this point. Now it's time to let go so that you can truly flow. Life loves you and supports you. You can live the lifestyle you desire (and are used to) while doing work that is fulfilling to you and that is in alignment with your soul's purpose.

Sometimes it's hard being a woman in a man's world!

As a Conflicted Chandra you sometimes feel torn and out of balance. This lack of balance is probably a result of not properly focusing your feminine and masculine energies. Perhaps you're a corporate Chandra surrounded by too much masculine energy, or a stay at home mom with not enough masculine energy. Either way, it's time to uplift your feminine essence and learn how to tap into your power so that you can balance better. After all, life does not have to be a juggling act.

WHAT YOUR ISSUES TEND TO BE

Depletion is your number one issue. Saying NO is your number two issue. You don't take enough time for yourself. It's time to say yes to YOU once in a while. You're so plugged in to work, family, and friends (not to mention everything else you're involved with), that you forget to unplug from everyone once in a while and plug into your true power source. You know you're a Conflicted Chandra when your girls call you up for a night out and you KNOW you really need to have some alone time, but you go anyway and end up having a terrible time (Was it worth it? After all, something inside of you told you not to go.)

WHAT YOU NEED MOST RIGHT NOW

You need to be OK with saying NO. Your primary focus needs to be honoring your truths and standing firm in your beliefs. You also need to appreciate your masculine and feminine energies, and know when and how to express them. Sometimes you don't want to do something (and that's OK). Let's end the conflict and learn to honor your truths.

*"If you don't define yourself for yourself then you will be crushed
into other's fantasies of you and eaten alive." -Audre Lorde*

The lyrics of Terrance Howard's song Shine Through It speak to your heart, Tuned Out Tracey: "All I want to be is a little bit more like me. And all I want to do is let some light shine through." As a Tuned Out Tracey you are ready to tune out the static and noise from everyone's radio station. You're ready to tune into your own frequency, play your own tune, and dance like no one is watching!

WHAT YOUR ISSUES TEND TO BE

Doing YOU is your number one issue. You want to do you, but you haven't clearly defined who YOU are for yourself. You've found yourself so attached to labels (mother, wife, doctor, coach, teacher, lawyer, soror, deacon) that you've forgotten who YOU really are without them.

WHAT YOU NEED MOST RIGHT NOW

You need to strip the labels away, one by one, and get to the core of who you are. It's time to step into your own power, activate your gifts, and live and love passionately. You need sacred spiritual practices that will keep you grounded and constantly remind you of who you are.

Many people want to uplift their life but either don't know where to begin, or lack the accountability to help them stay committed to change and growth. Let this book be the first step on your journey. It's time to infuse your soul with passion. You deserve to live a wonderful life. Life loves you and supports you. Are you ready?

The world desperately needs women to say YES to themselves. TRANSFORM your life! CULTIVATE your power within! LIVE with passion!

ON YOUR MARK. GET READY. GET SET. LET'S GROW!

Whether you are a Playing It Safe Portia, Conflicted Chandra, Tuned Out Tracey, or a woman ready to say YES to herself, the concepts I present in this book will give you practical steps to cultivate your power within. My 6-step Uplift System is based on the Universal Laws and designed with ease for you to apply to your life daily. The steps make up an acronym that is easy to remember: UPLIFT!

UPLIFT SYSTEM

Step 1: Understand

Step 2: Poise and Position

Step 3: Love

Step 4: Intuit

Step 5: Faith

Step 6: Trust

Improving the quality of your life requires that you commit to incorporating these 6 steps into your life daily. Consistency is the mother of change. In order to be uplifted, you've got to rise up! You've got to show up and do the work. This system works, if you work it!

STEP 1: UNDERSTAND

Understanding is the first step toward freedom and peace.

EXPLANATION

The first step to uplifting your life is to understand your role. Life doesn't happen to you, it happens because of you.

We set our own limitations, and perhaps there are limiting beliefs that have manifested in your life as situations or circumstances that you do not desire.

You can heal and change your life with the basic understanding that your thoughts are powerful. Things that you believe to be true will manifest in your life, and they will be in alignment with that truth, desirable or not.

Remember that all beliefs are true to the person who believes them. Limiting beliefs show up as roadblocks in our life, stopping us from living the life we desire.

What have you accepted as truth in your life?

REFLECTION

This reflection will allow you to see the truth of what you believe right now. Holding a mirror to your life is not always easy (after all, who wants to accept the fact that they believe they are not worthy of fulfilling friendships?). There are three steps to this reflection.

1. Explore your beliefs about yourself and various areas of your life by writing what you believe to be true about each of the following topics: your time, your money, your relationships, your health, how others view you, women, men, your current life situation. For example, as it relates to your time you may say "I believe there is never enough time in the day". Be honest with yourself. Nothing you believe is wrong.

2. Review your list and answer the question: "Which limits have you put up in your life?"

3. List 13 things that you want more of in your life.

INFUSION STEP

Pay attention to times that you feel strong emotions such as love, hate, admiration, or jealousy. Observe your thoughts for a period of time (perhaps you will choose a day, Thoughtful Thursday, for example, or a week of awareness). As you notice a thought, ask yourself what you are believing to be true with that thought. If that thought is not in alignment with the things you desire, then choose a different thought, right in that moment This step will require a lot of patience and practice.

AFFIRMATION

I am willing to grow and change.

Be ready for your prosperity.

EXPLANATION

You deserve to be prosperous in your time, your relationships, your finances, and every aspect of your life.   This second step requires that you begin to do the work to change your situation.   To do the work you must unlearn limiting beliefs and create empowering beliefs for yourself and your life.   When you are poised, you go beyond taking ownership; you command the situation.

One way to quiet your mind of limiting beliefs is to ask questions.   Rather than resorting to blame or anger about a situation, simply ask "What is this?".   When you feel angry at someone you feel has wronged you, ask "How can I be loving in this situation?".   If you find yourself sulking in money worries, simply ask "How can my gifts and talents create money for me?".   When you ask a question, the answer will always be revealed to you if you are open to receiving what you need to grow and change. This willingness to grow and change positions you for prosperity.

REFLECTION

This reflection exercise will help you release your limitations and be empowered by writing what you desire in the affirmative as a belief.   Review your list of beliefs from the reflection in STEP 1.   As you read each statement, think about what you want to be true instead.   For example, if your belief about relationships was that "People intentionally withhold information from me", then you might want people to be more open with you, in which case your empowering belief is "I am committed to being open in my communication with others".

INFUSION STEP

Keep your empowering beliefs with you in your mind, heart and in your purse. Focus on them daily for about 10 minutes of uninterrupted time.   Say them aloud. Revisit your empowering beliefs during moments of low vibration (i.e. feeling bad, jealous, envious, angry, resentful, etc.).

AFFIRMATION

I can change my thoughts.

STEP 2 REFLECTION

Find the good and love it.

EXPLANATION

Love is the stimulus for good in your life. A very dear friend of mine always says 'find the good and praise it'. When you look for what is good, you change your perspective of a situation. I believe that your perspective of a situation will bring you closer or further away from uplifting your life.

Finding the good is finding love. If there is a blockage in your life, preventing you from having what you desire, you must open your heart to more love. Blockages are the result of fears. Love and fear cannot co-exist. Love is joy and when you are in joy, you are in love. Love is all there is. You have committed to doing the work, and now you must enjoy the journey of healing and growth.

REFLECTION

Find a space that makes you feel comfortable and safe. You want to be uninterrupted for at least 40 minutes. Perhaps you will find time to do this reflection before retiring for the night, or early in the morning before everyone rises. Your space may be during a lunch break of solitude, or a Friday evening at home in your favorite chair over a cup of tea. During this time, I want you to list the things you love. There is no order of magnitude with what you can love. You may love the sounds of guitar strings, or the smell of patchouli. You may love when your boss compliments you, or when you are able to throw a party everyone enjoys. List as many things as you can during the 40 minute reflection time.

INFUSION STEP

Practice being in love. Remember that love is joy. Be in joy! And enjoy being in joy! Find things that you love and express them as affirmatives. For example, if you love your sister's laugh because it lifts your spirits, then say "I enjoy my sister's laugh".

AFFIRMATION

There are so many people, places and things for me to love. Today I choose love.

STEP 3 REFLECTION

You already know all you need to know.

EXPLANATION

The great philosopher Ernest Holmes said that "intuition is spirit knowing itself". You are well equipped to uplift your life from where you are to where you want to be, because all you need is inside of you. It's time to lift it up and bring it to the surface!

You already know what you need to know. Perhaps there is something that you are pretending not to know. If you are willing and ready to grow, then you must allow this Spirit to reveal itself through you.

You must listen to your heart, your head and your hunch. Intuition is always there to support you, but you must work it so that it will work for you.

REFLECTION

Recall and list the times that you had a knowingness that proved to be true. Examples of knowingness are feelings that you should do something and the situation works out for the better, or hunches about things that led you to further discovery or growth. Think about how your intuition spoke to you, and how you felt. These will be keys to further growth.

INFUSION STEP

Intuition is like a muscle. In order for it to be strong, you must strengthen and train it. For the next week, whenever there is a challenge or situation for which you need clarity, simply ask with passion for your intuition to help you.

AFFIRMATION

I trust that all I need to know is being revealed to me at the right time for my highest good.

"Faith is the evidence of things not seen." -The Bible

EXPLANATION

Faith may be the evidence of things not seen, but what do you see with your imagination? If the things you desire were not ready to be real in your life, then they would not exist within your imagination.

We live in a world of infinite possibilities. Everything that has ever happened can happen again, and the things yet to happen are waiting for someone through which they can manifest.

Dare to imagine all that is possible for what you desire in your life. Have you set limitations on your desires? If so, then you have not exercised full faith.

You can't put your faith in doubt and expect your desires to manifest. You can't put faith in poverty (i.e. through limiting beliefs) and expect prosperity.

Just as you can intuit, or allow spirit to reveal itself through you, you can demonstrate faith by allowing spirit to work through you.

REFLECTION

List one thing that you desire and all of the ways that it can manifest. Allow your imagination full reign of your mind as you explore the possibilities. Be as silly, creative and imaginative as possible.

INFUSION STEP

Einstein's greatest theories began as wild imaginings. Allow yourself "Einstein moments" of imaginative play in your mind. Review your list of desires from STEP 1 and explore the possibilities of how they can manifest. Do this during increments of daydreaming throughout your day.

AFFIRMATION

I love and trust my imagination. I enjoy the creative process.

STEP 5 REFLECTION

Let go so that you can grow.

EXPLANATION

Trusting requires that you let go of your need to control how and when things will work out. Your only responsibility is to simply get clear about your desires (what) and intentions (why), and let life handle the where, when and how.

Trust is a demonstration of faith. Mistrust breeds worry, and worry either takes you back to a past experience, or to a future that has yet to happen. Worry is rooted in fear. When you mistrust, you fear that things will not go the way you want.

Often times, what we want comes in a way we did not expect. The only expectation you need is that your faith will result in the fulfillment of all of your desires.

You are a unique individual, created to express all of your uniqueness. Life is full of resources, support, and love to guide you. Trust that this is so.

REFLECTION

Recall a time when you were mistrusting of a person or situation. What were you afraid would happen if you put complete trust in this person or situation? What was the worst that could happen if you released control? What were you worried about?

INFUSION STEP

Be mindful of thoughts that take you away from the present moment in an unhealthy way. For the next week, make a conscious effort to stay in the present.

AFFIRMATION

I am in the process of trusting life more and more each day.

(Note: Replace the word 'life' with whatever fits your situation.)

STEP 6 REFLECTION

Congratulations on making the decision to uplift your life! Remember the steps of my Uplift System and incorporate them into your life.

Step 1: Understand - What limits have you set? What are your truths?

Step 2: Poise and Position - Unlearn limiting beliefs and create empowering beliefs for yourself and your life.

Step 3: Love - Open your heart to more love and break down blockages of fear.

Step 4: Intuit - Listen to your heart, your head and your hunch. Allow Spirit to work through you.

Step 5: Faith - Believe in possibilities. Allow Spirit to work through you.

Step 6: Trust - Let go of your need to control how and when things will work out.

I encourage you to uplift a sisterfriend by sharing this Soul Infusion Guide. Here are a few ideas:

- Gift someone with a copy of this book.
- Post a comment about it online at a blog or website.
- Tweet about it. Post a link to this book on a social network.

I would love to connect with you! I am transforming communities– one woman at a time. I work with women ready for change. I welcome you on this journey.

As you consider hiring and experiencing me as your teacher and coach, please make sure you've visited my website at www.fenesha.com for an overview of the services I provide. If you feel that I'm the support you need, then complete my Let's Get Acquainted Form. I will read your responses and contact you for a complimentary introductory assessment session. After that, we'll determine what is the best fit for where you are on your life's journey.

To your uplifting,

Fenesha
www.fenesha.com
get@fenesha.com

Thank you for being you.